Poetry Bouquet

Susan McCray

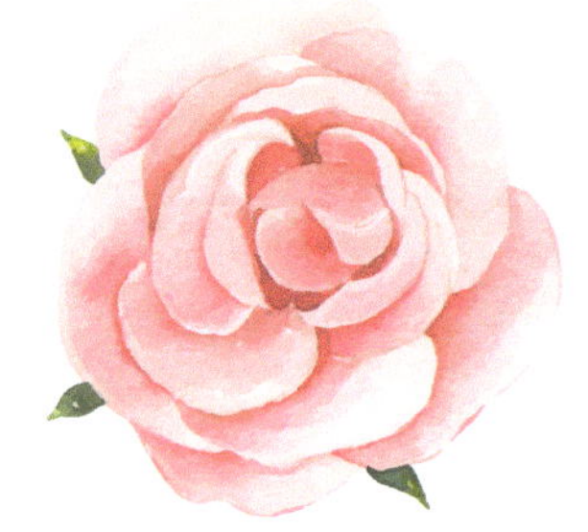

ISBN: 978-1-78324-305-1

I dedicate this book to the creative artistry and love to the most important people in my life – My parents who inspired me Franceska and Harry and the love of my life Kent

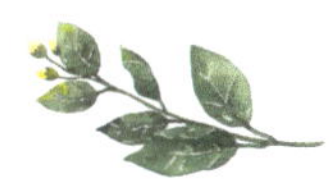

Franceska

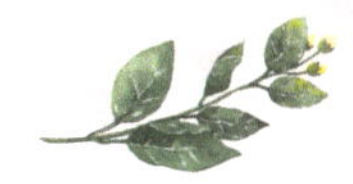

By Susan McCray

Her flawless face
time can never erase
A Graceful pose In her stunning clothes
Her music she would compose
The art she created and chose
And She'd love to Point her toes

Her love of dance
Her dreams of romance
Creative style her beautiful smile
Would light the room as a flower in bloom

A creative genius everyone would agree
She'd make all smile with glee
Love of turbins and hats she wore and
Large rings on her graceful hands galore

the sensitive way with care
She shared her talents with an honest flare

known as the twinkling starlet in her radio prime
in my eyes and heart
will always shine

My best friend my confidant my incredible mom
With her beauty and talent putting others to shame
A beautiful Woman Franceska is her name

Two Left Hands; Self Portrait

By Franceska

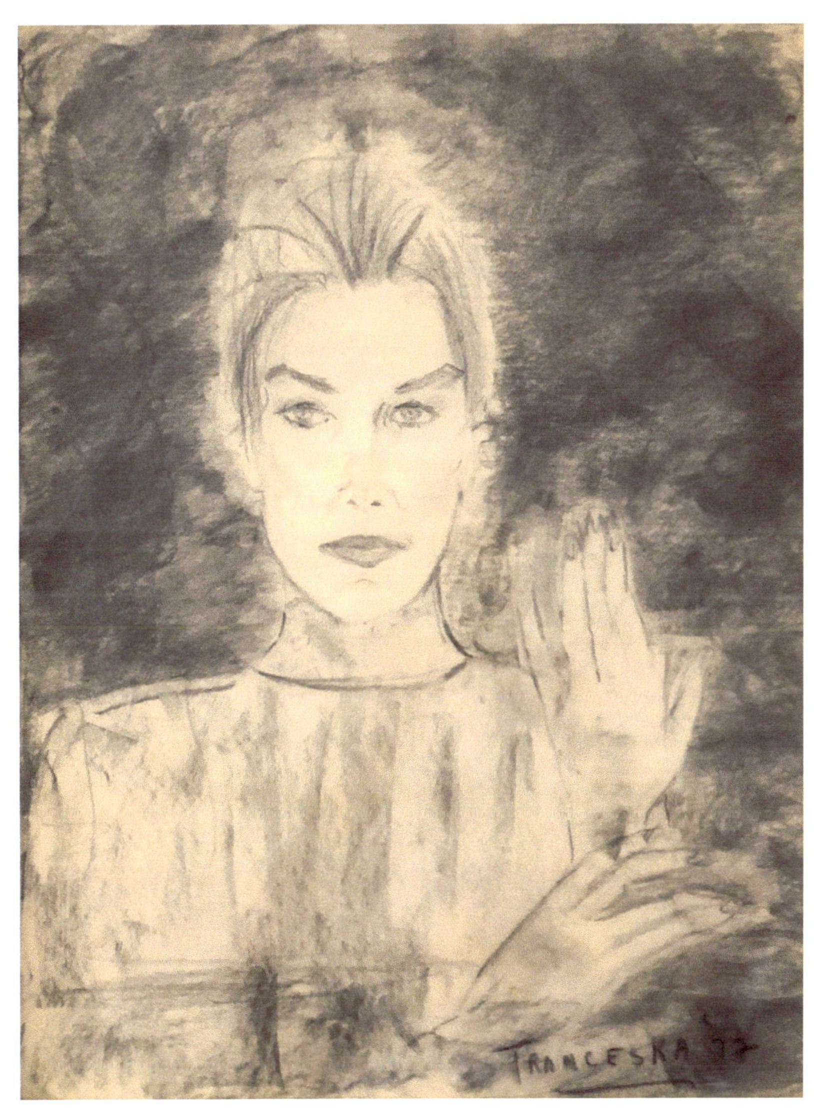

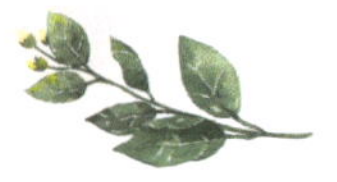

A Memory of You

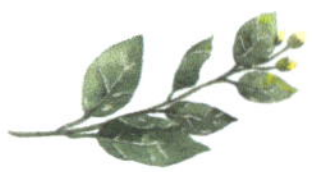

By Susan McCray

The waves of an ocean so deep
Delving into emotions that reap

Sorrow and tears of all the years
That were spent in yearning glory
Yes this truly paints the story

A mood of blue upon the water
With a glimmer of hope throughout light
Could the moon in all its splendor
Bring happiness within your sight

The ocean moves so steady and calm
A stroking brush within your palm

Emotions are so clear in view
This painting of blue a memory of you

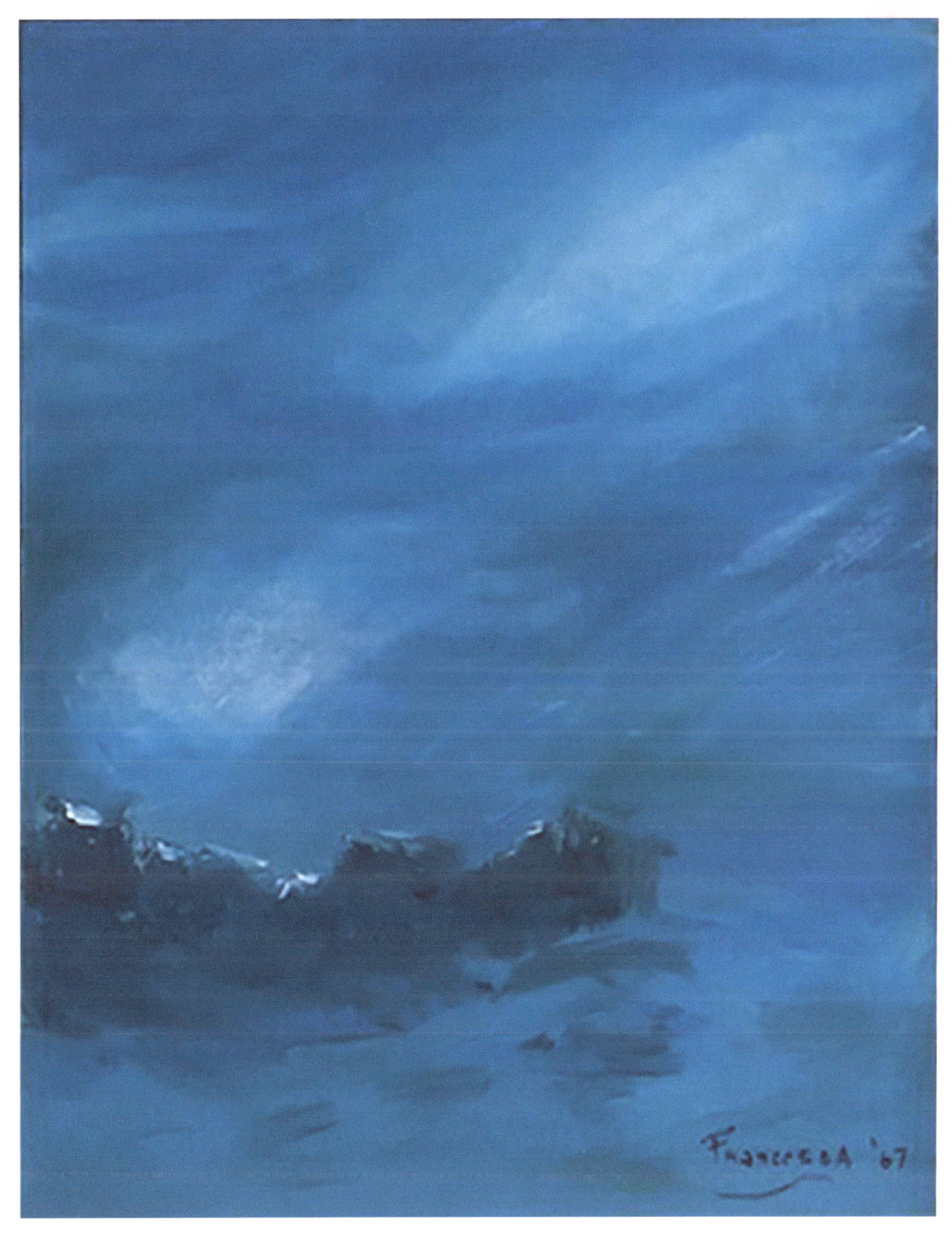

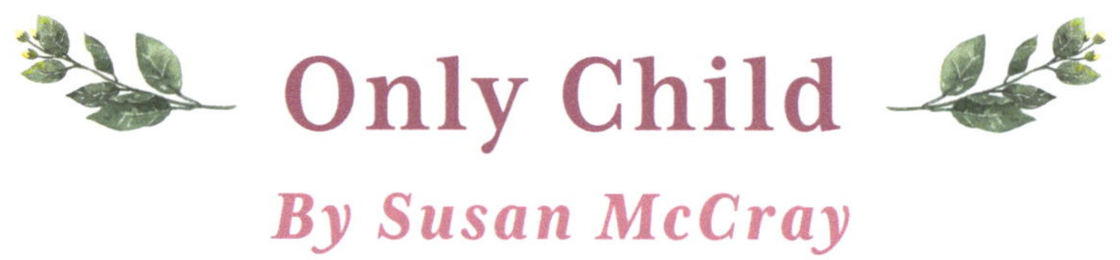

Only Child

By Susan McCray

People think I'm spoiled being an only child
But its far from being the truth
Being the one and only can sometimes feel
Pretty lonely in your youth

Others thought me lucky there was no other
I just had my dad and my beautiful mother

I grew up quickly the childs table just didn't work for me
Spoke like a grown up and sat like a lady
I would hear my parents say
I feel badly she won't have another so she could play

When we're older she'll be alone
But I'm grateful I was happily married no children of my own
They are now all gone and yes I am alone

But as I think back I guess i was spoiled
Being the only child
With three important special people I had
My man my mom and my wonderful dad

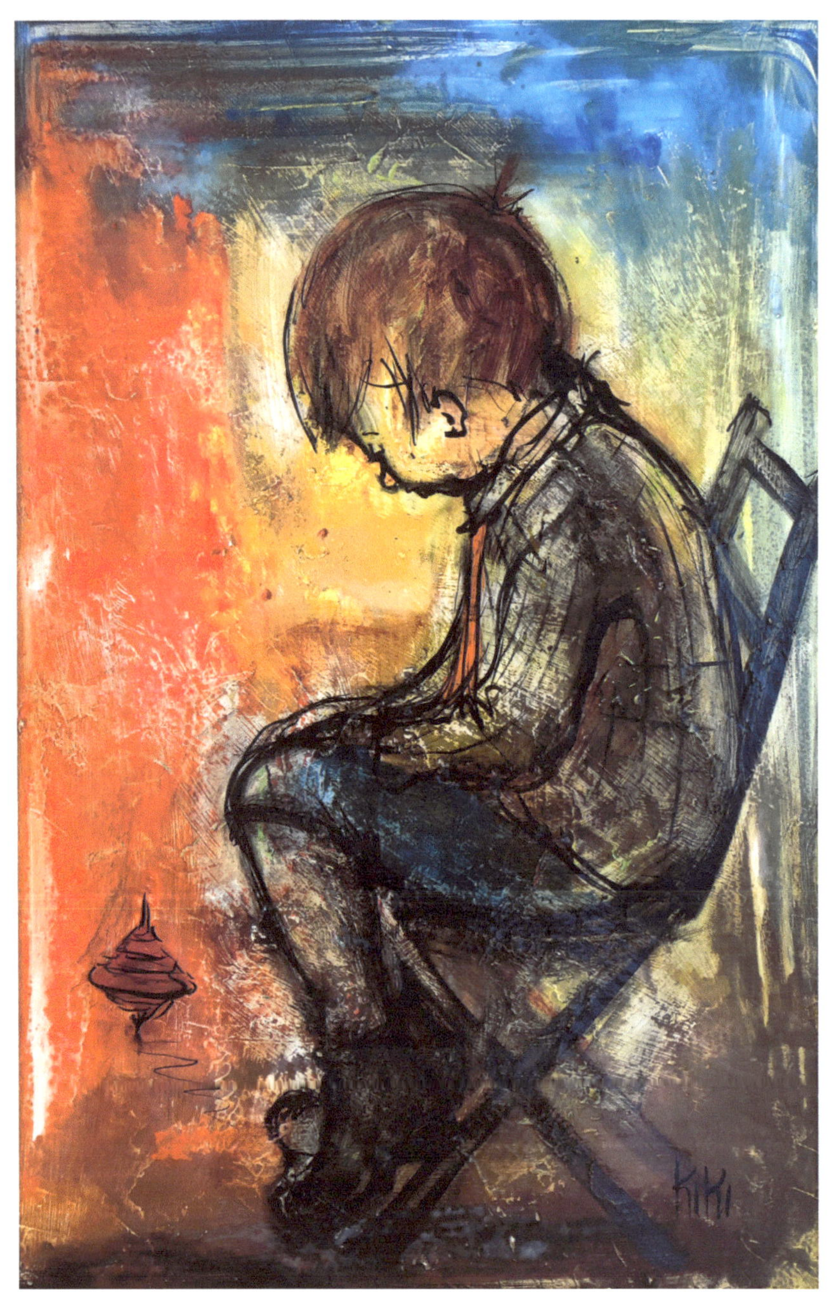
KiKi

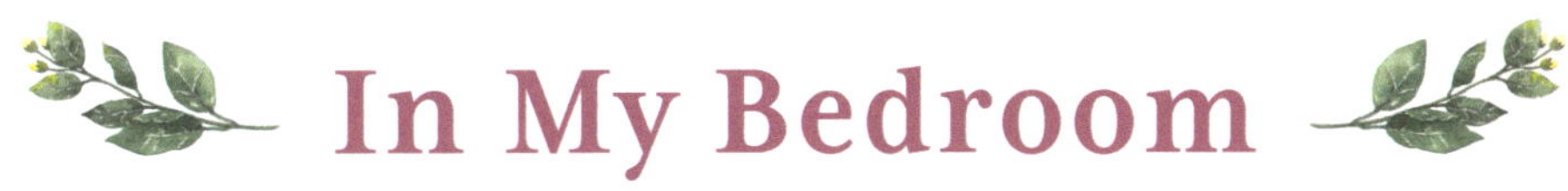

In My Bedroom

By Susan McCray

A rose sits alone on a desk in my bedroom
Like the woman who sat before it
In her prime and in full bloom

The petals like her skin so flawless
The perfume of her being so sweet
Should this be a memory of beauty
Or reminder of a lonely heartbeat

The yearning to remember a graceful pose
Enhancing the beauty of the rose
Even with care and love abound
It still felt like no one was around

The time where does it fly
The hours and years have gone by
As we know beauty is not forever

And must leave to be reborn another day
As in the life of the lonely woman
Reaching out in her own graceful way

Now there are only fallen petals
Of the rose once in full bloom
on the lonely desk In the corner of my bedroom

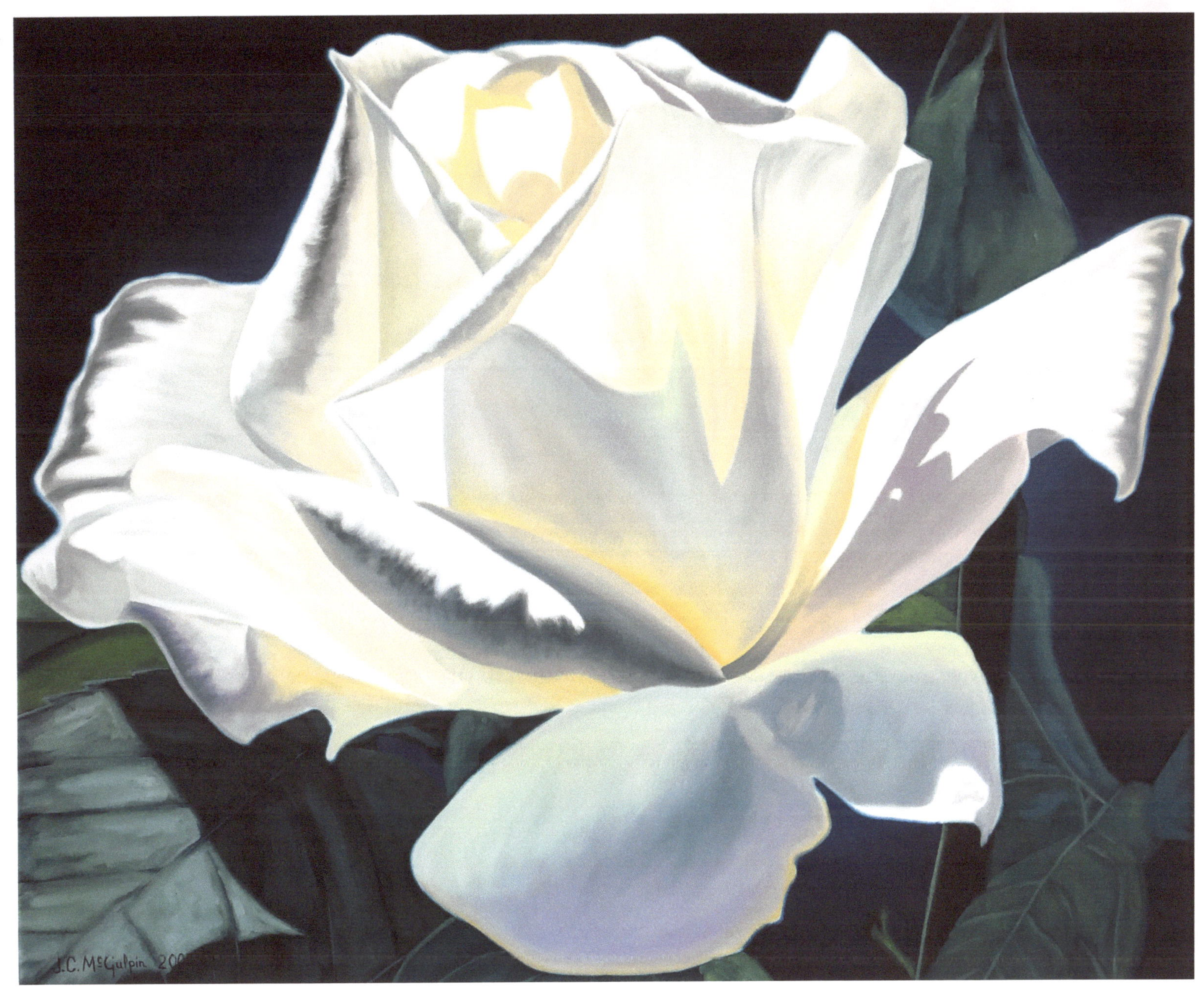

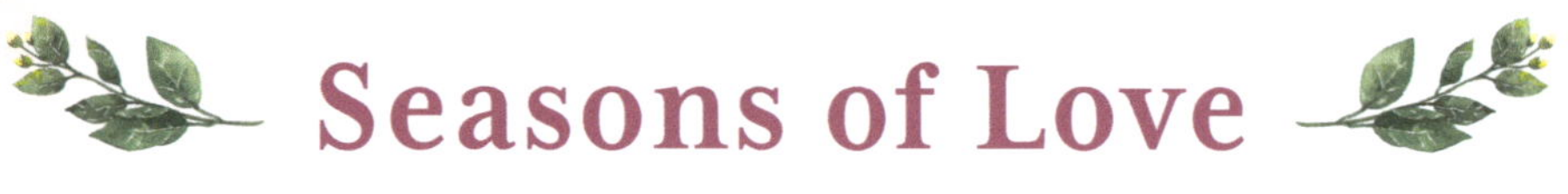

Seasons of Love

By Susan McCray

Love begins like the days of spring
It makes you warm and makes your heart sing

Sandy beaches by the ocean blue
Special moments we all look forward to

Then the warmth of the sun becomes cool
And we no longer sit by the pool

The leaves have turned to yellow and brown
And the love we felt is beginning to frown

Then it starts all over again the yearning for
Another chance
To find another new seasons' romance

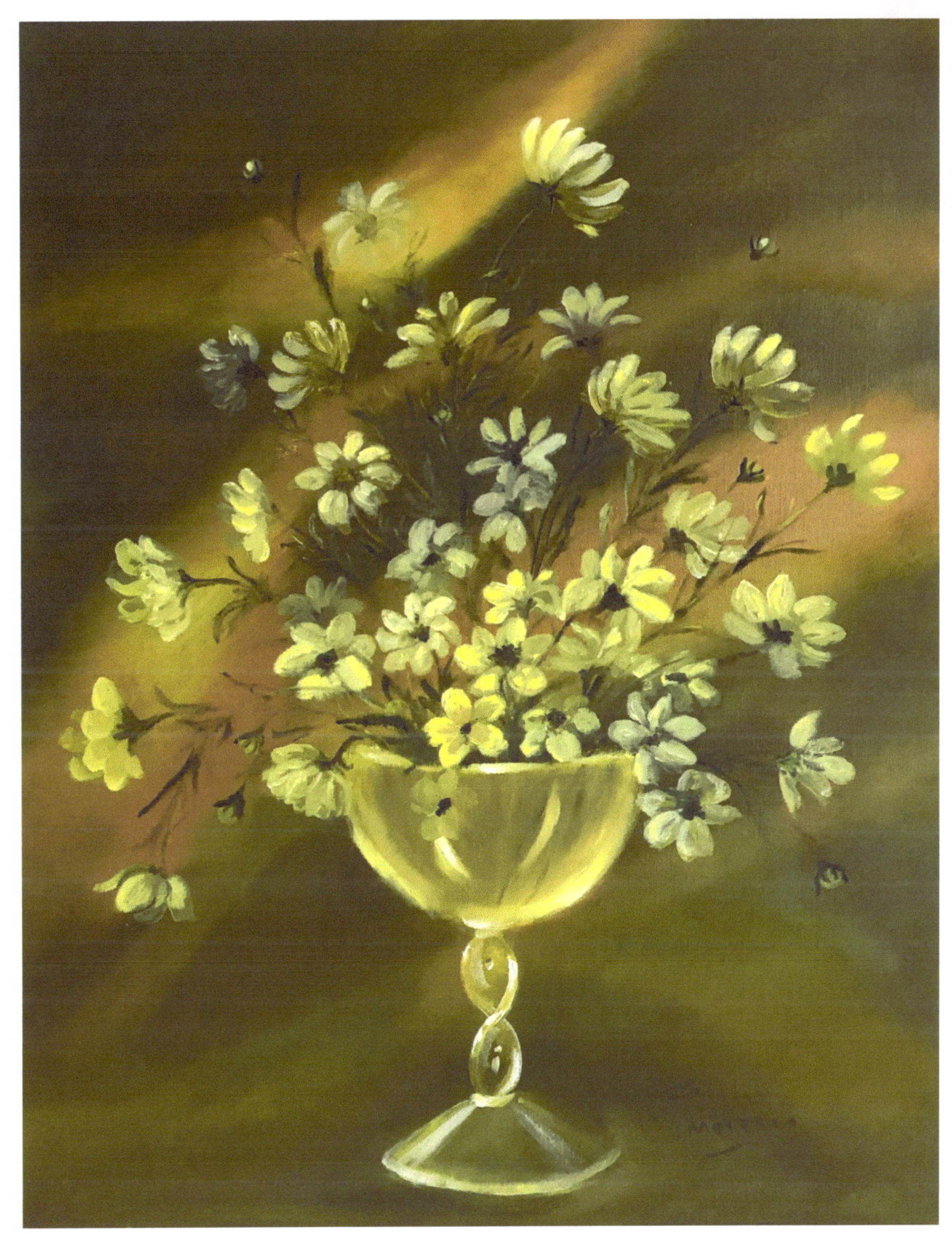

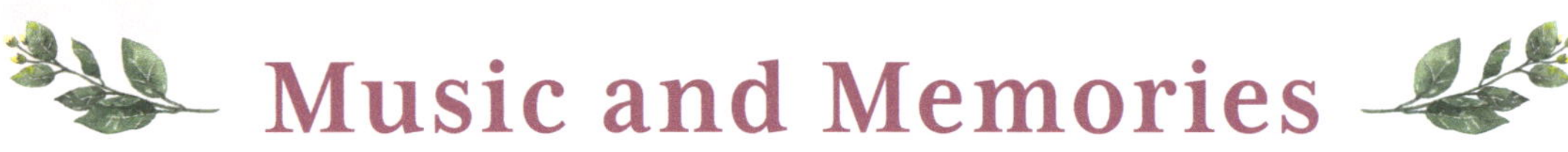

Music and Memories

By Susan McCray

Music can make us feel glad or even make us a little sad
It can bring back memories good or bad

One thing on which we can all agree
Music can fill the heart with glee

Friends you may have lost in the past
Are found with melodies and will forever last

All your experiences new or old
Become special memories as treasures of gold

Though music may bring back some pain
When hearing a simple and fervent refrain

Humming a melody all the while
Can also bring on a special smile

We can't forget when we hear a tune
Whether in the car or in a saloon
In a reaturant, market, or in a waiting room

We are surrounded with many thoughts galore
Music keeps our memories alive forever more

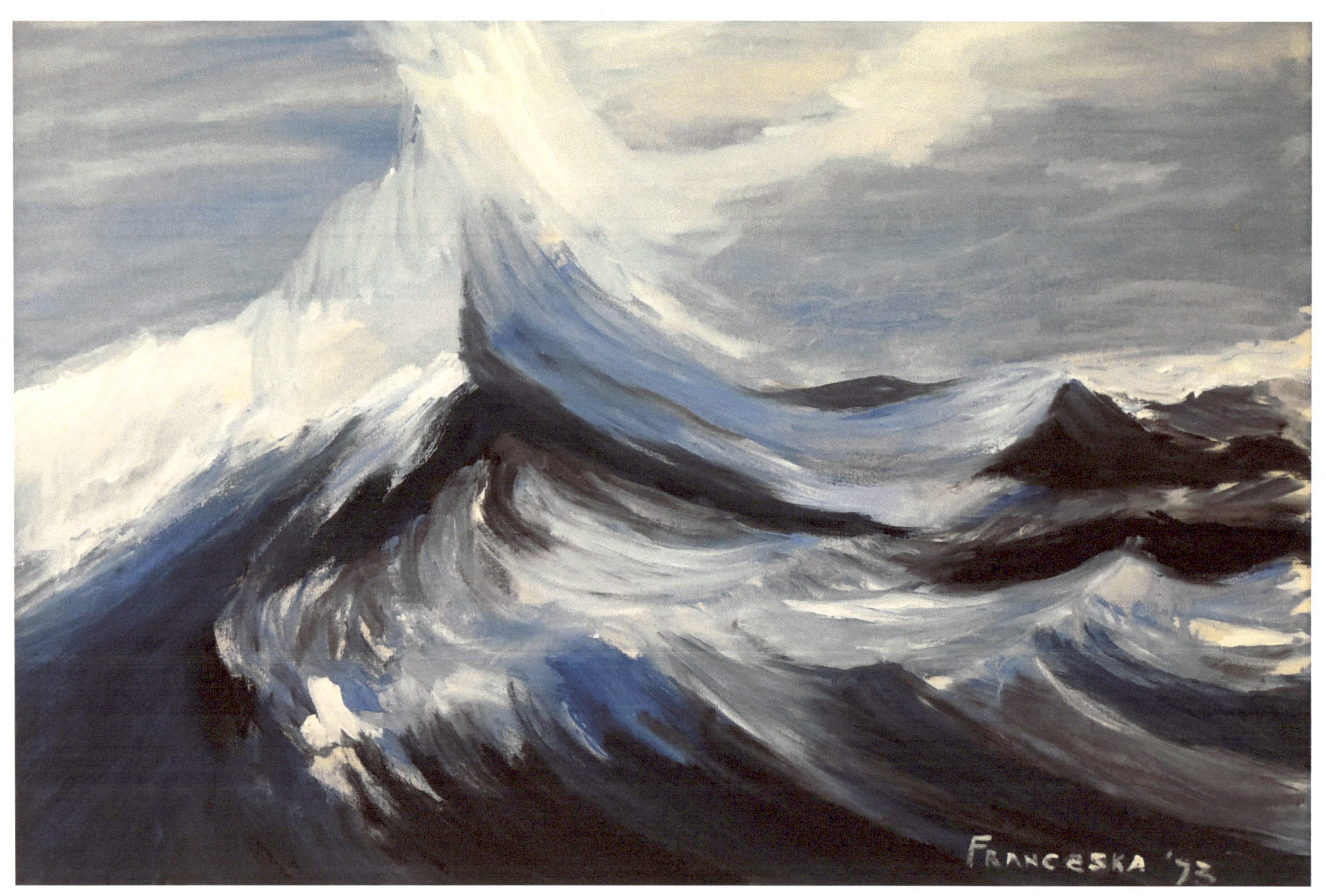
FRANCESKA '93

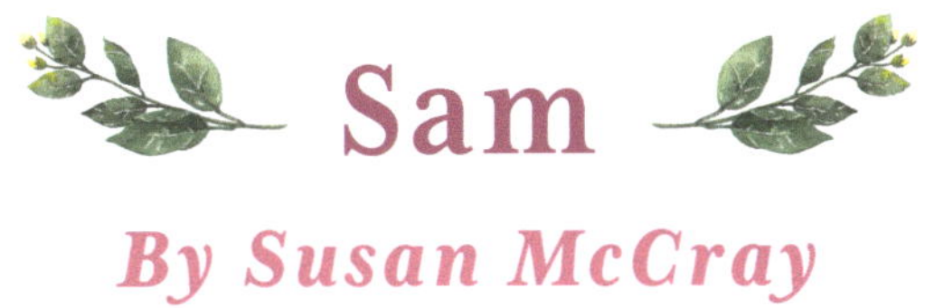

Sam

By Susan McCray

He's the special puppy I knew I should choose
And never thought I'd ever lose

No one can ever replace
His beautiful warm and caring face

Loved me whether I'm sad or glad
Thinks I'm beautiful when my hair is wet and straight
Or when its set with big rollers he thought I looked great

He loved me when I shared my food
Or when I'm in a lousy mood

Under the windowsill he'd lay his head
Next to my side of the king size bed
So smart and clever I'll always remember

Chasing that little red ball
On the wood floor down the hall

Chewing and devouring that rawhide bone so fast there's no way in
The world it would ever last

Looking like a king over there
Sitting in his favorite black leather chair
Or when he'd jump up between my feet
With his hind legs hanging over the ottoman seat

He loved to be next to me
Watching whatever was on tv
He seemed to know what I was thinking
As he looked at me with his bright eyes blinking

Mornings while the coffee would brew he'd stretch then shake my
Hand on cue thats what he really loved to do

Those little things he never would forget
Probably cause he knew the cookie he would get

When we'd leave the house
And tell him to be a good boy
He'd look sad and put his head down near his favorite big yellow toy

When we got home opened the door with our key he'd be right at the
Door tail wagging with glee then he'd whimper with gladness and
Joy and bring us his favorite yellow toy

When it was warm and we thought he'd come out to be cool he was
Always fearful of the swimming pool

We'd yell in the house and say come out bring the ball and play but
Inside the glass door he preferred to stay

The look we would get always seemed to say
Me come out to the pool you must be kidding no way

The special love we had is hard to explain
In my heart it will always remain

Now even the house feels alone
He's not here to chew on the bone

Or to toss his red or yellow ball
So he can find it upstairs or chase down the hall

He was so smart and oh so very clever
My devoted friend Sam – the dog I will love and
Remember forever and ever

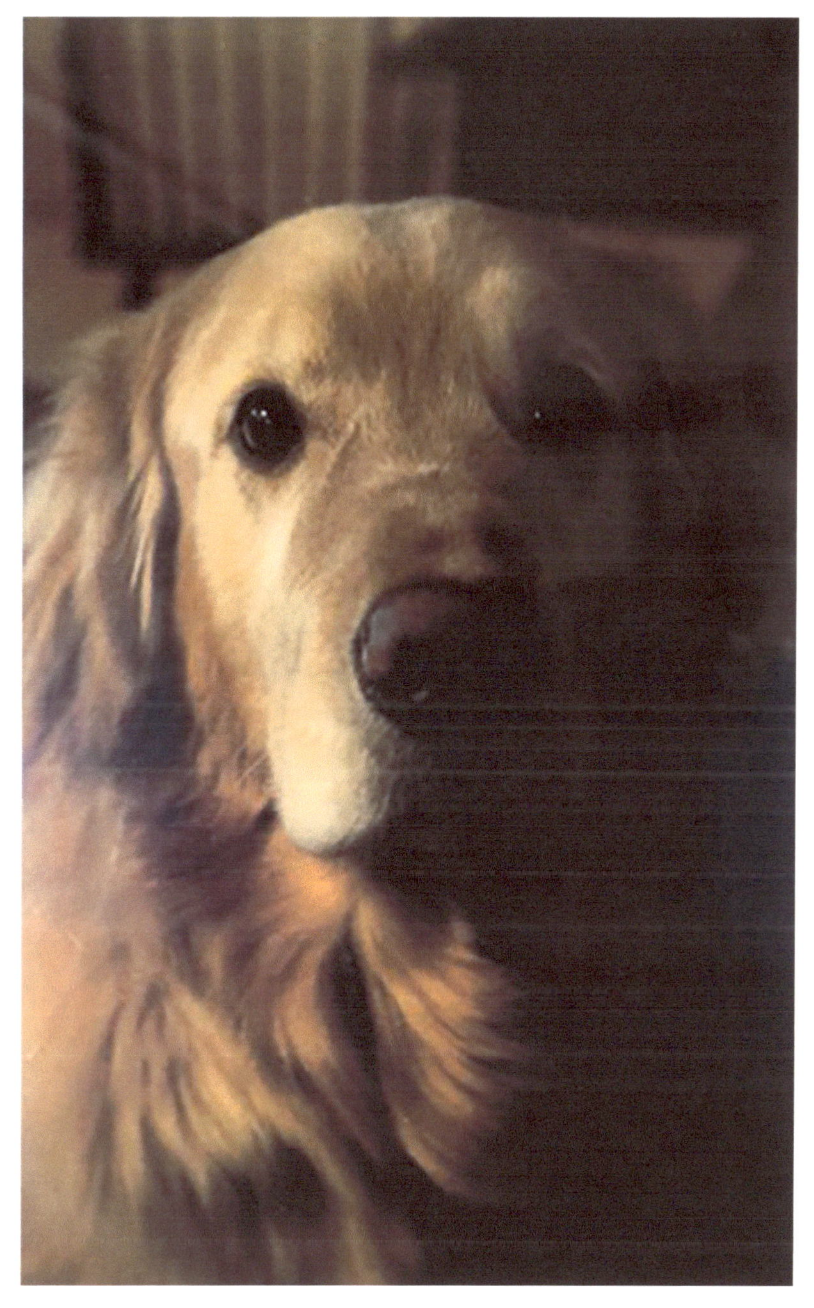

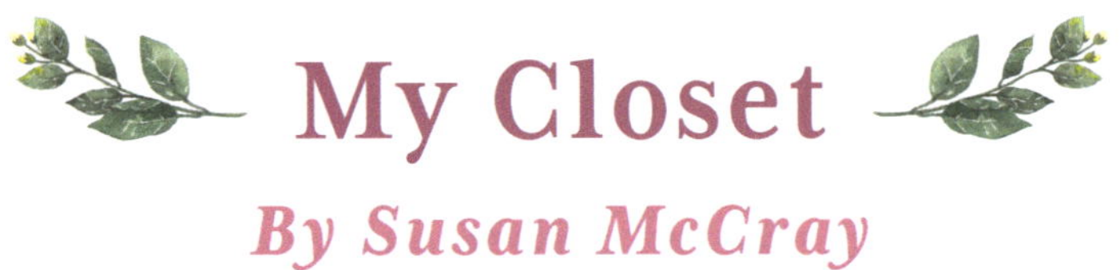

My Closet

By Susan McCray

I'm about to open my closet door
And start to give away things I used to adore

There's that yellow dress, when I bought it
I really liked it, I guess
The style is bound to come back
I don't think I'll throw it in the sack

Oh, here's my prom dress
I wore it long ago
How can I possibly ever throw?

There's always room to hang it in the back
A cummerbund, full skirt, and spaghetti straps

And the five pair of jeans I purchased on sale
I'll get into them some day, that's a minor detail

The bright pink jacket I truly pined for
By a famous couture designer

Why didn't it ever go with anything I had
That always made me feel quite mad
Now I remember, a personalized letter marked
Merchandise alert – it read we're sorry

We sold out of the matching skirt

The black hat I really love, why don't I ever wear it?
It goes with everything I have
One day I will, I swear it

Here's the white blouse I love so well I don't think anyone can really tell the collar
has a very light stain inside my jacket

It shall remain

On the shelf a special box
Containing stockings and a collar of faux fox if I strike a certain pose
When I wear these pantyhose

The runs will barely even show
Ive decided they don’t really have to go

I cant give some of these shoes away
Even the odd ones really must stay the tinted red satin
Or the white heel patent

The stiff gold sandal that kills my toes

Or the black silk shantug with the blue bow
I certainly cant throw any of these
Especially the stretch boots that go past my knee

And look, my favorite pink nightgown Ive worn so many times
Even with the frayed lace and worn sleeves

To throw out would be a crime

I’ve become quite possesive of things I ought to give a way I think I’ll clean my
closet on some other day

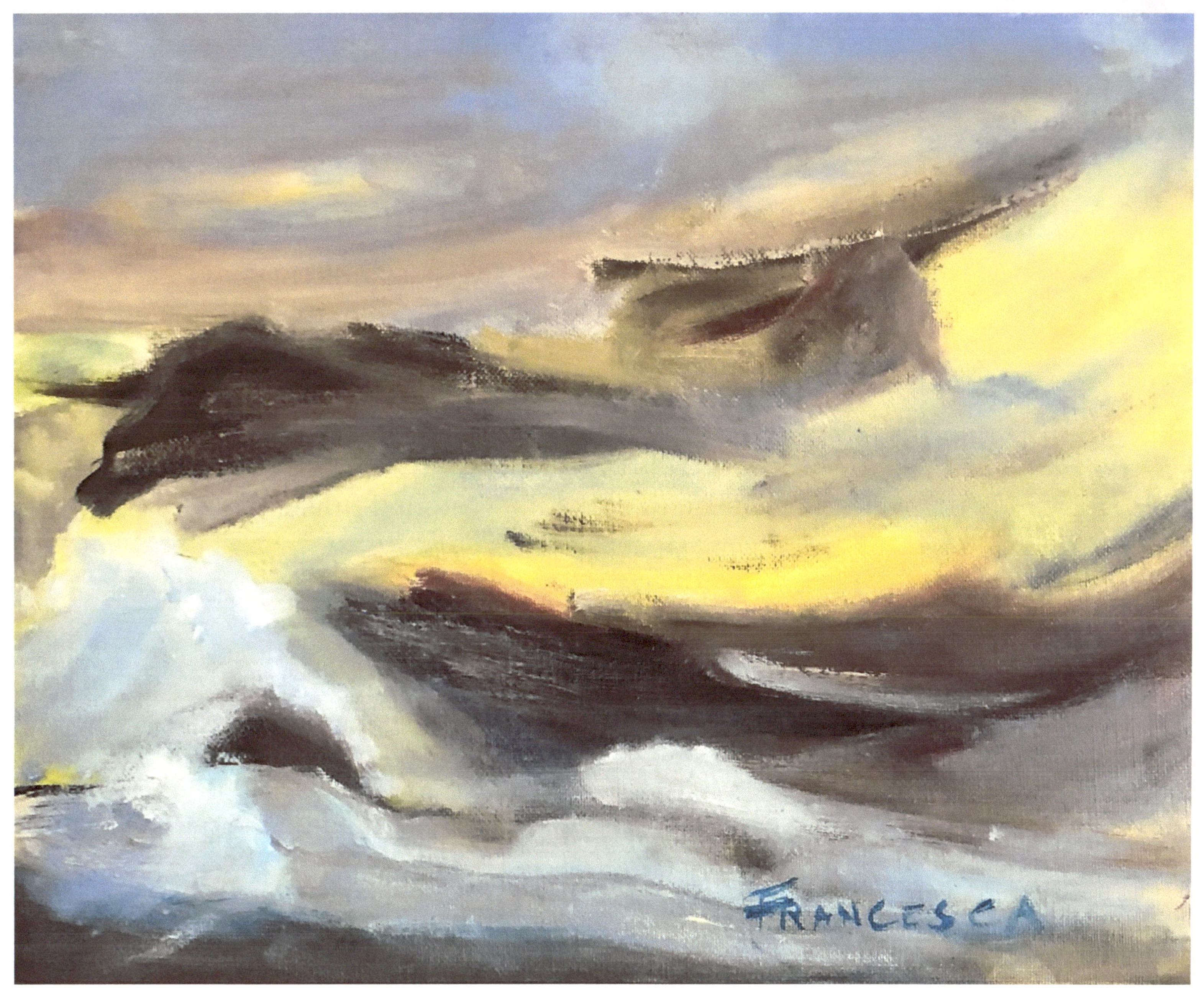
FRANCESCA

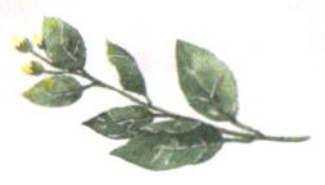

To Vacuum or Not to Vacuum

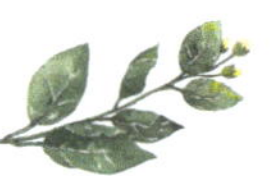

By Susan McCray

Do you have any rugs in your home- most people do
In the master bedroom and in two guests rooms they lay
Which means to vacuum is not necessary every day

It never ceases to amaze me
Our long time cleaning lady
Brings out the vacuum to make its wretched noise daily

The vacuum when put away each day
Is in the closet in the entry way

But out it comes every morning without any warning

The rugs napp is definetly wearing
Each day the vacuum starts blaring

I asked please don't run the vacuum today
And was glad to hear the silence in play

What is that pounding I'm beginning to hear
I think it's the sound of my couch pillows I fear

The covers are being taken off of them to clean
And being thrown in the washing machine

I hope they don't turn out like my favorite jeans fit
They've shrunk so much they don't even fit

Well another day has finally passed
The house clean and quiet at last

Her car just drove down the road
Now its quiet in my lovely abode

Looking forward to the sounds of sorrow
When the vacuum runs and shes here again tomorrow

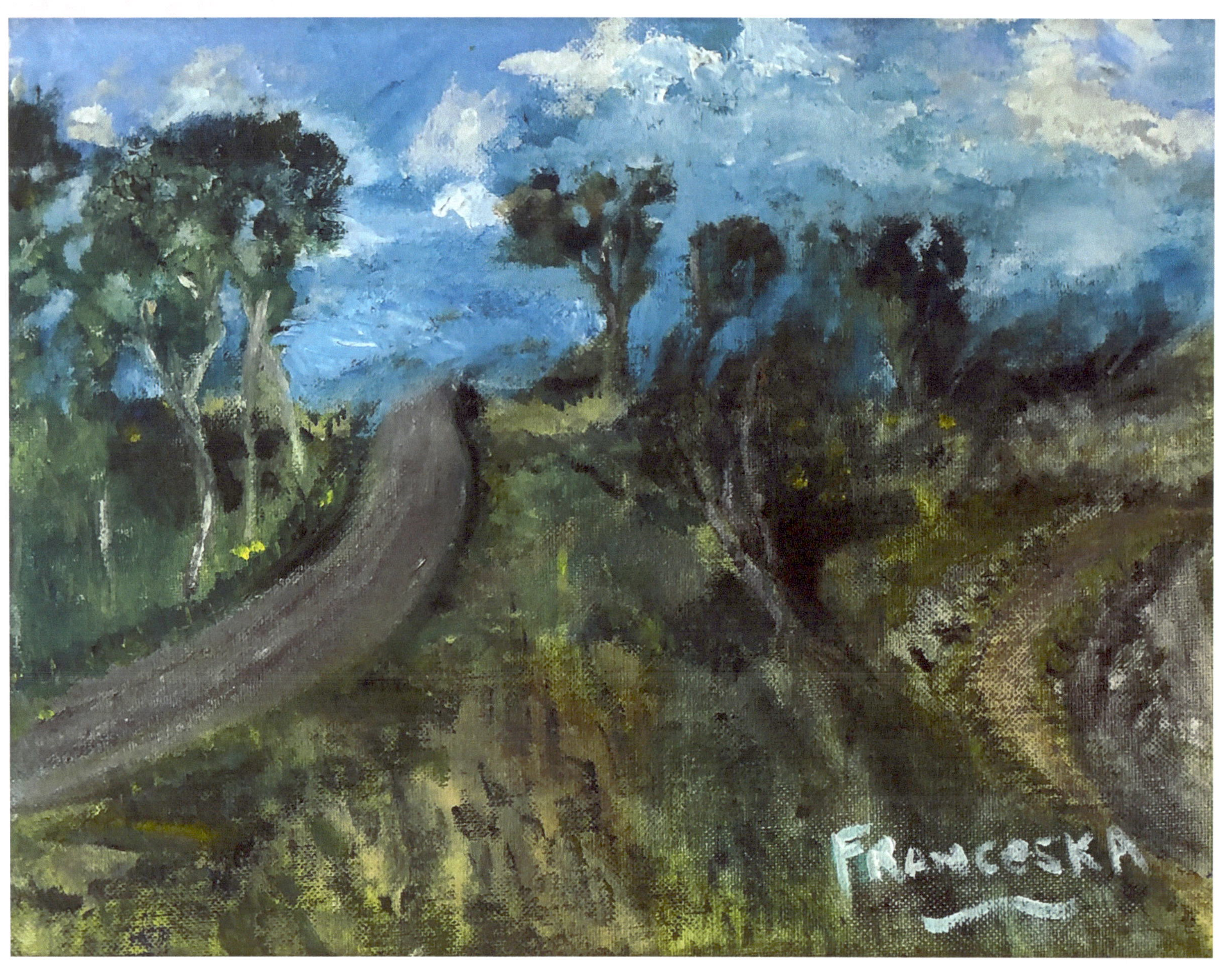
FRANCESKA

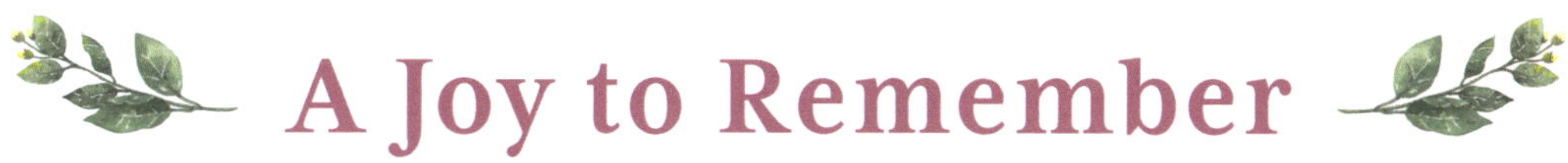

A Joy to Remember

Poem by Maggie Brown

Francesca ruled a special Kingdom
It was filled with pink carnations, pink balloons, and dolls with sweet faces.
Stuffed animals were painstakingly dressed in fashionable fancy.
Occasionally there was a piece of sinfully rich dark chocolate.

Her treasure room was a closet filled with back issues of Vogue.
(it would make her laugh and brag just a little when "fashion" would finally catch up to her wardrobe)
An inspired hat was her crown
Her flawless skin accentuated with dynamic jewelry.

She had been kissed by the Muses of Music and Art
From Childhood, she could spin music into gold
She could capture the beauty of the world with a brush stroke
Perhaps she received these gifts because she was so good at sharing them

Or perhaps because her innocence protected them
In the early days of radio, she reigned-
"WBBM, Chicago – bringing you Lee Frances, The Twinkling Starlet"
Fans praised her talent. She won their hearts.
But that was another time, one adventure in a lifetime of many.

She was cherished by Harry, her king.
And today, Francesca Paley Sukman is joyfully remembered by her daughter.

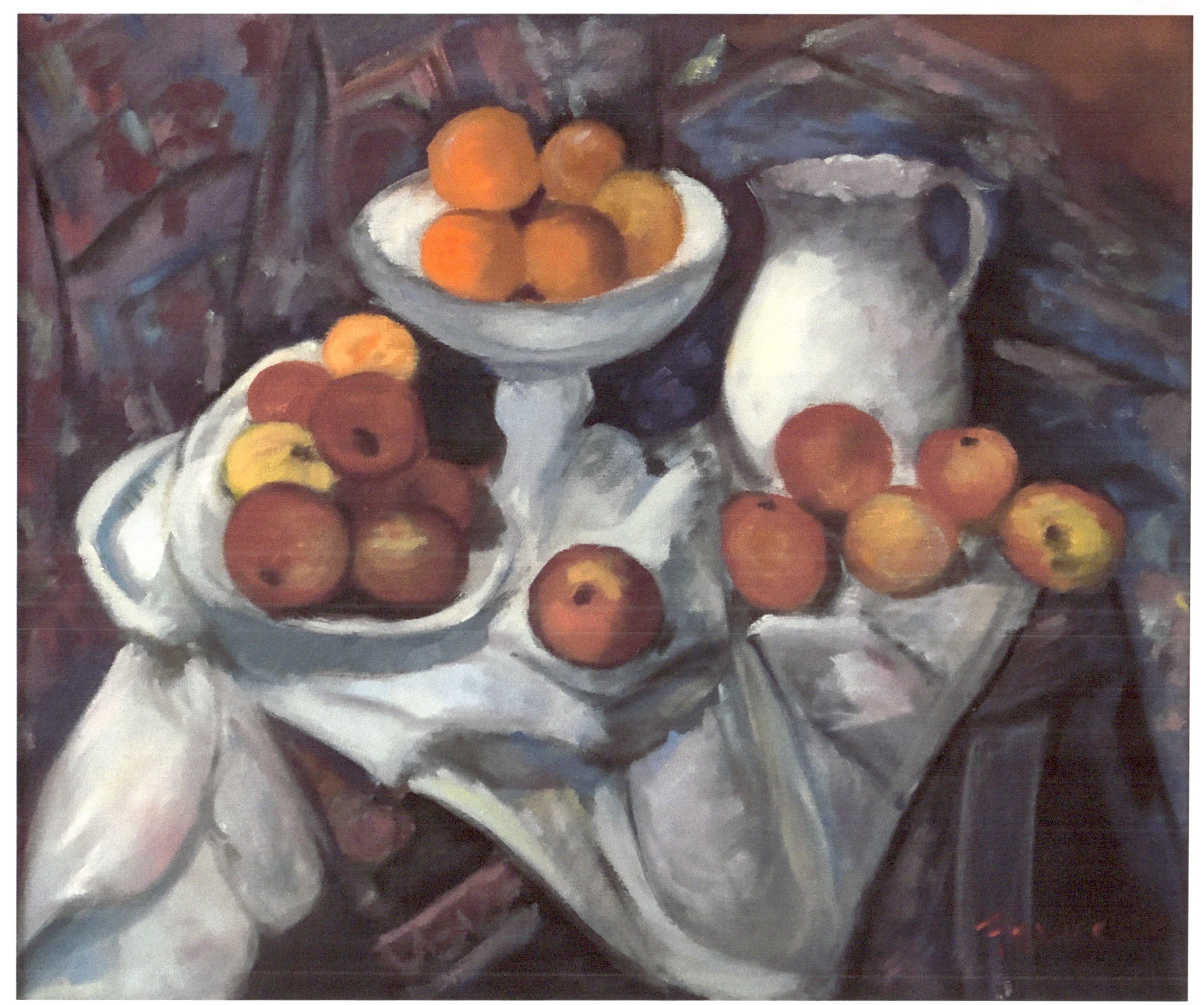

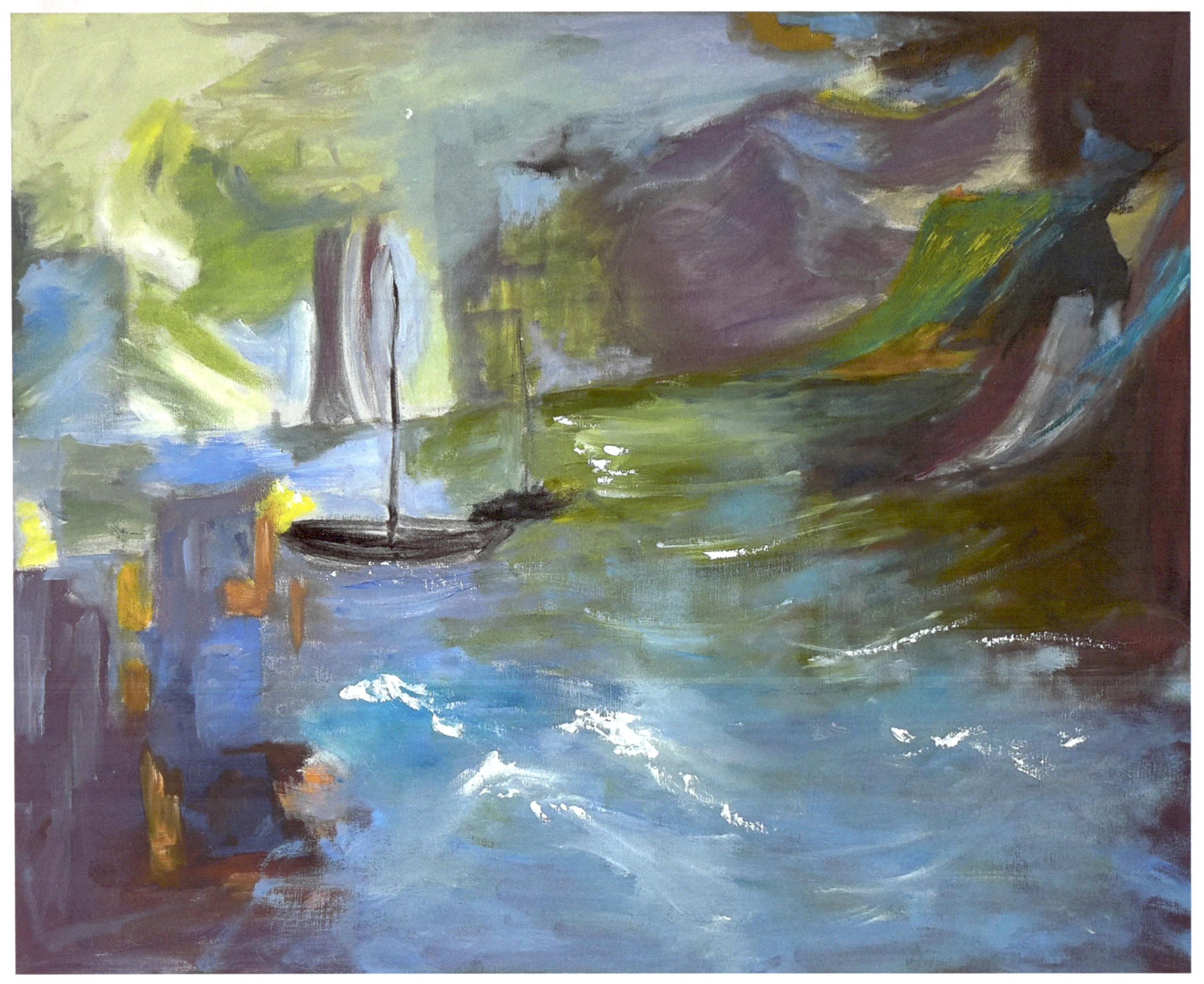

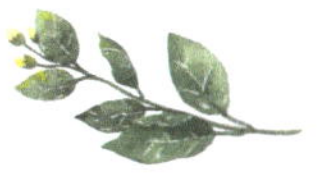 Francesca Paley Sukman 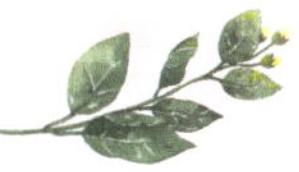

A Biography

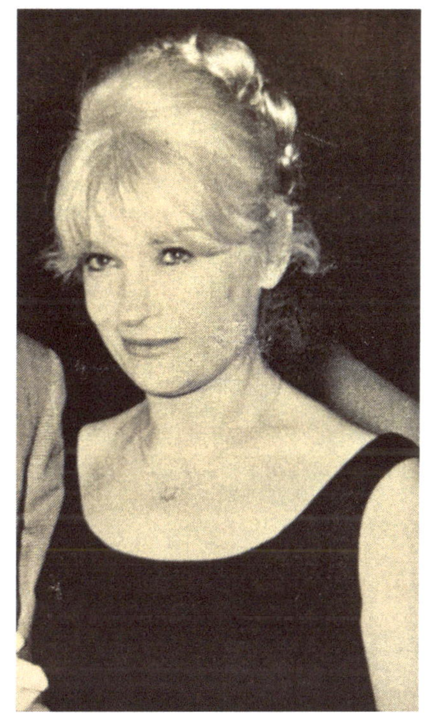

Francesca was called a "musical genius" by the most famous composers of our time; Victor Young, Max Steiner, Alfred Newman, Meredith Wilson, Harry Warren, Sammy Fein, and the list goes on and on. She was born in Chicago. Her inclination and talent for music was evident: she was able to play at performance level at age four. Remarkably, she played everything she heard by ear, to the amazement of everyone, including her composer/pianist husband Harry Sukman. He would practice difficult classical pieces for hours. Francesca would sit down minutes later and play it back to him. It baffled him when she would sometimes even play it in a different key then originally written.

She began formal music studies at the American Conservatory of Music in Chicago. When still in her teens, she joined the staff of the Columbia Broadcasting System in Chicago, as pianist and organist, under the name of Lee Frances. She wanted to prove to herself and others she could get this job without using her well known family name, Paley.

Her associations at CBS and Mutual were lengthy. Millions of listeners knew her programs and the background music she provided for countless soap operas from coast to coast.

Francesca was gifted in the allied arts: poetry, art and ballet. As a member of ASCAP, she composed music, including several beautiful themes for television. Professionally, her time was devoted to appearances on network and local shows, as well as recording albums.

While working at WBBM, she met her future husband, Harry Sukman. They moved to Los Angeles in 1947, where he became a renowned two time "Oscar" winning composer for motion pictures and television. Francesca chose to give up her career to raise their daughter, Susan.

In April of 1990, Francesca Paley Sukman died of ALS, (better known as Lou Gehrig's Disease). Her daughter Susan, a well-known casting director and producer, honors her mother's memory every year, by giving a luncheon awards event FRANCESCA's FASHION FANTASY, to benefit those affected by Amyotrophic Lateral Sclerosis (ALS).

The love and devotion between Susan and her mother Francesca, lives on throughout this day.

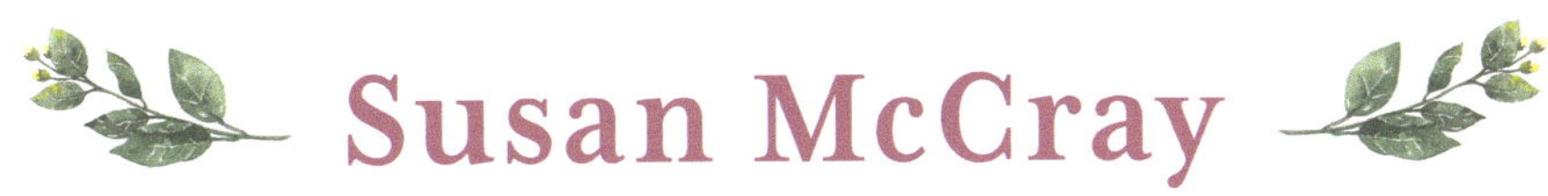

Susan McCray

A Biography

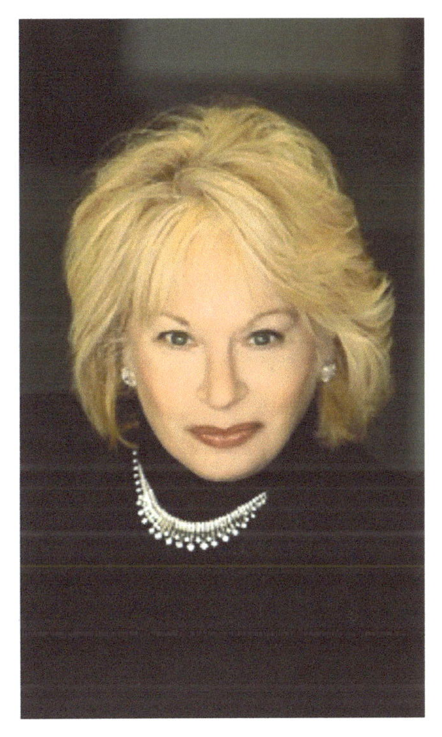

This book of poetry is Susan's fourth book, she is also a children's book author.

Susan has written the delightfully whimsical "Paddy Platypus" and also "The Story of Sammy & Zelda". She also wrote the inspiring story "Harry's Piano", based on the early life of her father, Academy Award Winning composer and concert pianist Harry Sukman. She is currently producing an animated film based on the book.

As Vice President of Talent for Michael Landon Productions, Mrs. McCray was the casting director of many acclaimed episodic television series including Little House on the Prairie, Father Murphy, and Highway to Heaven. She also cast the television movies The Diary of Anne Frank, The Loneliest Runner and Where Pigeons Go to Die. During her amazing career, she cast numerous shows for NBC, CBS, and PBS.

As a producer, Mrs. McCray's credits include the celebrated documentaries "Michael Landon: Memories of Laughter", "Remembering Kent McCray: Laughter Love and Television"; and "Don Collier: Confessions of an Acting Cowboy". She also produced the CD "Warm Heart Cool Hands", which is a compilation of some of her father's Academy Award-winning music.

Currently, Mrs. McCray is producing and hosting the podcast Kaleidoscope, airing on *mixcloud.com*, and also airing on radio station KJEWL. She is also the creator and host of the syndicated radio feature Hollywood Hotline.

Susan McCray's humanitarian spirit embodies passionate support for her favorite charities. She frequently organizes, produces, and serves as Mistress of Ceremonies for a variety of fundraising events, she is currently an "advocate" for KidsPlay Children's Museum in Torrington, CT.

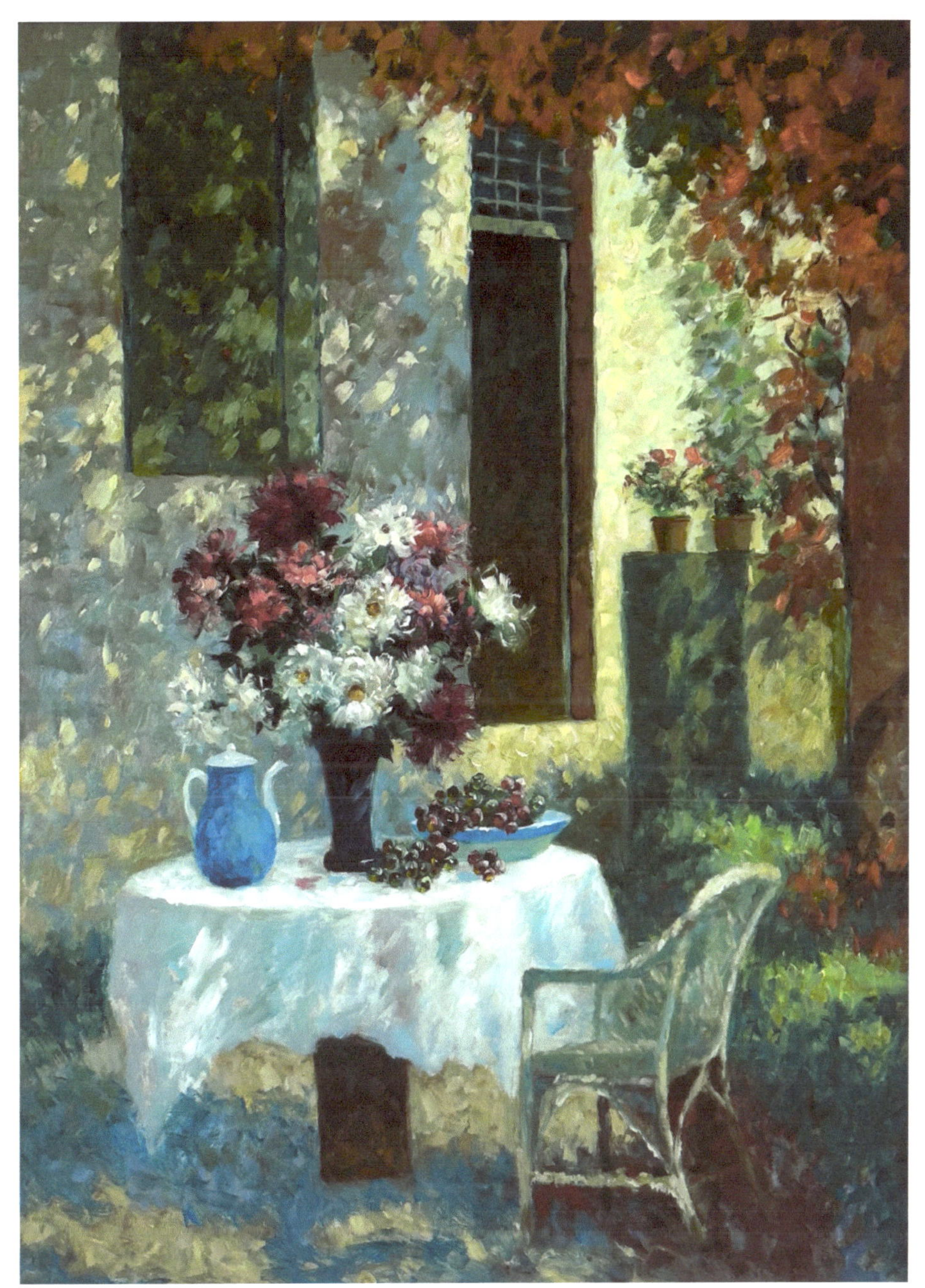

www.ingramcontent.com/pod-product-compliance
Lightning Source LLC
LaVergne TN
LVHW072329100826
845154LV00009B/144